The Lord's Prayer In Mandarin

Colouring Book

The Beautiful, Simple to Colour Characters
of the Chinese Language

主祷文 主禱文禱告

彩色画图本

MAGDALENE PRESS

The Lord's Prayer in Mandarin Colouring Book
The Beautiful, Simple to Colour Characters of the Chinese Language
by Esther Pincini

主祷文 主禱文禱告
彩色画图本

Copyright © Magdalene Press 2016

ISBN 978-1-77335-107-0

No part of this publication may be reproduced, stored in a retrieval system, or transmitted in any form or by any means, electronic, mechanical, photocopying, recording or otherwise without written permission of the publisher.

Magdalene Press, 2016

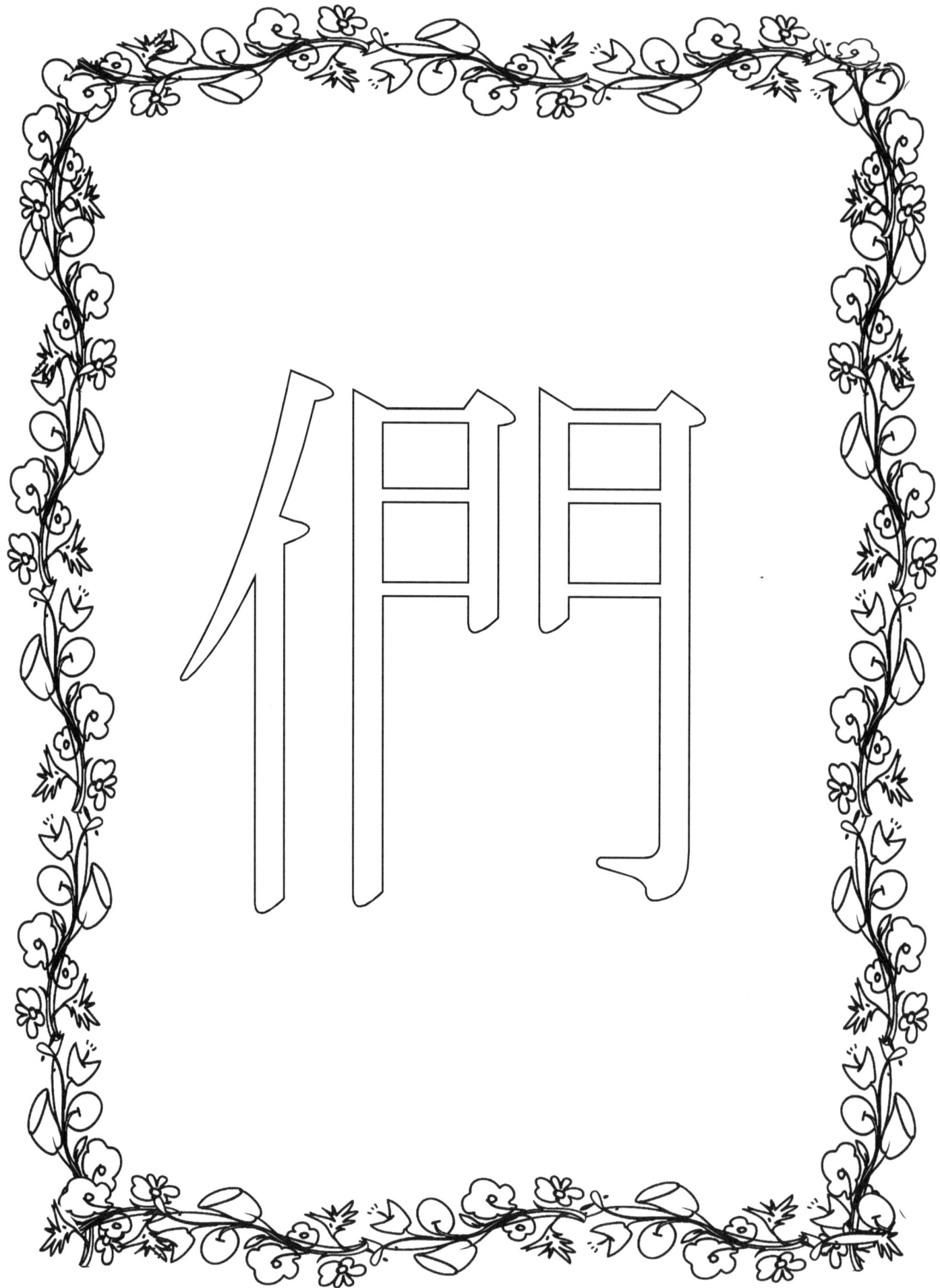

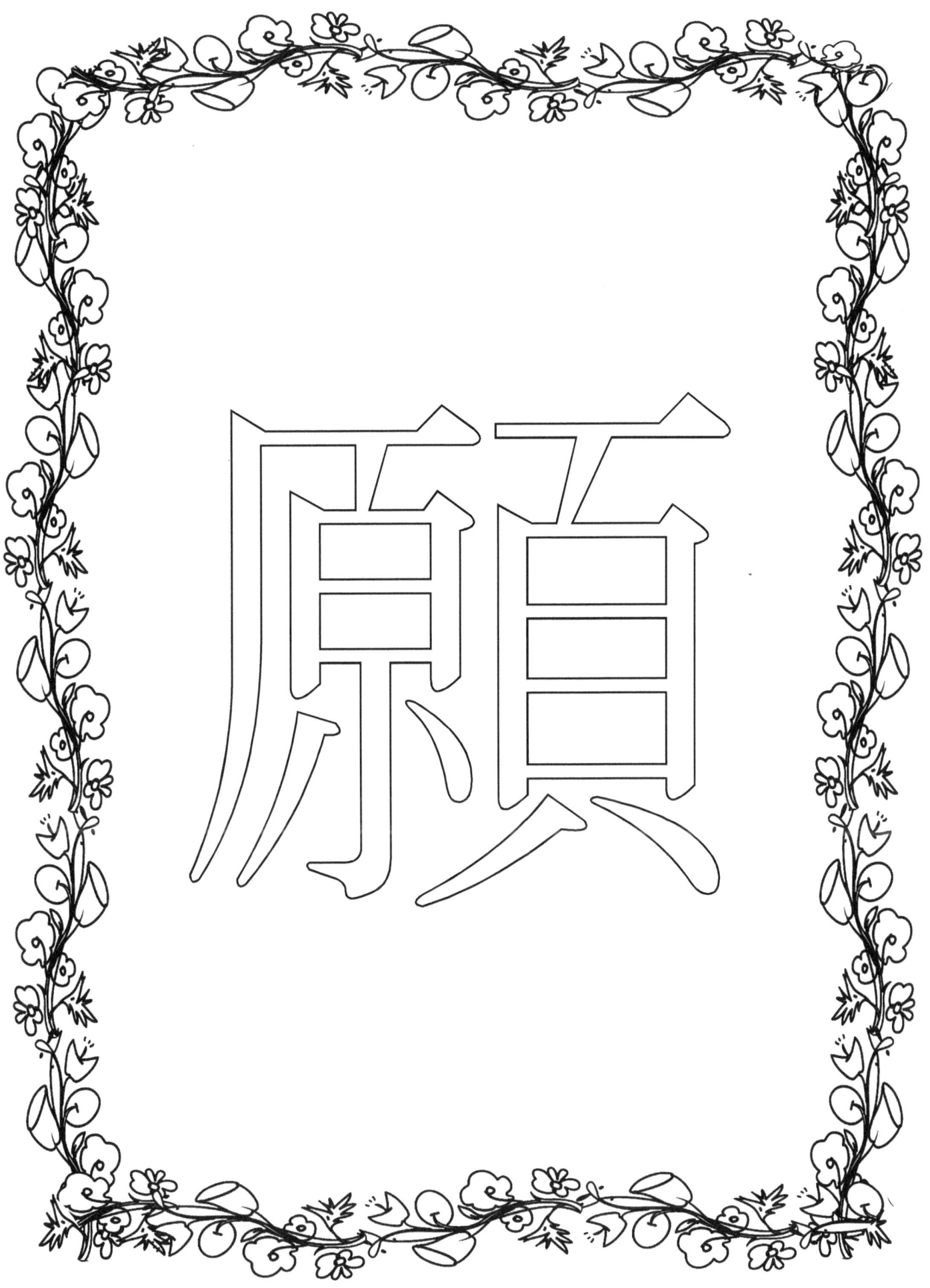

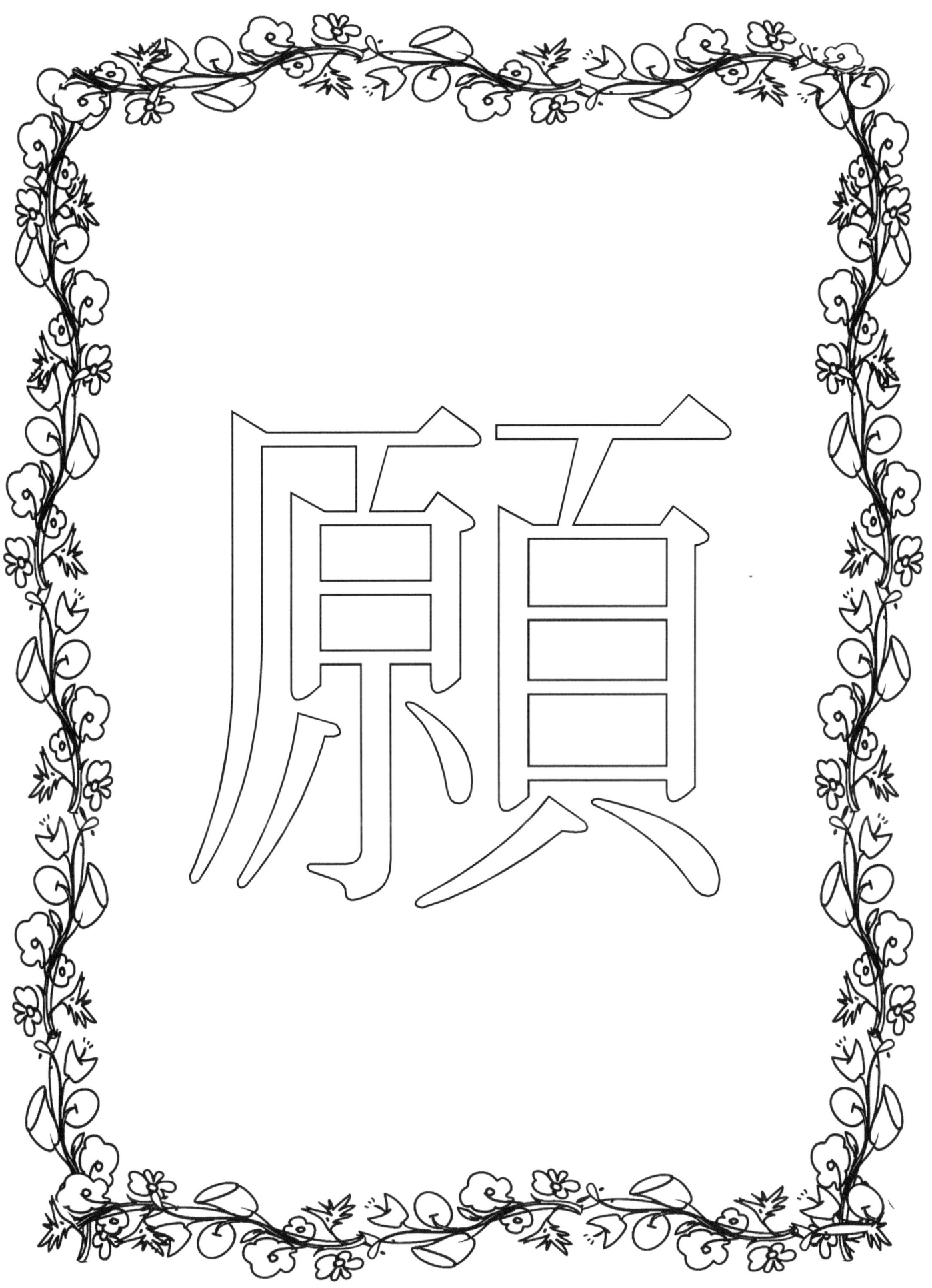

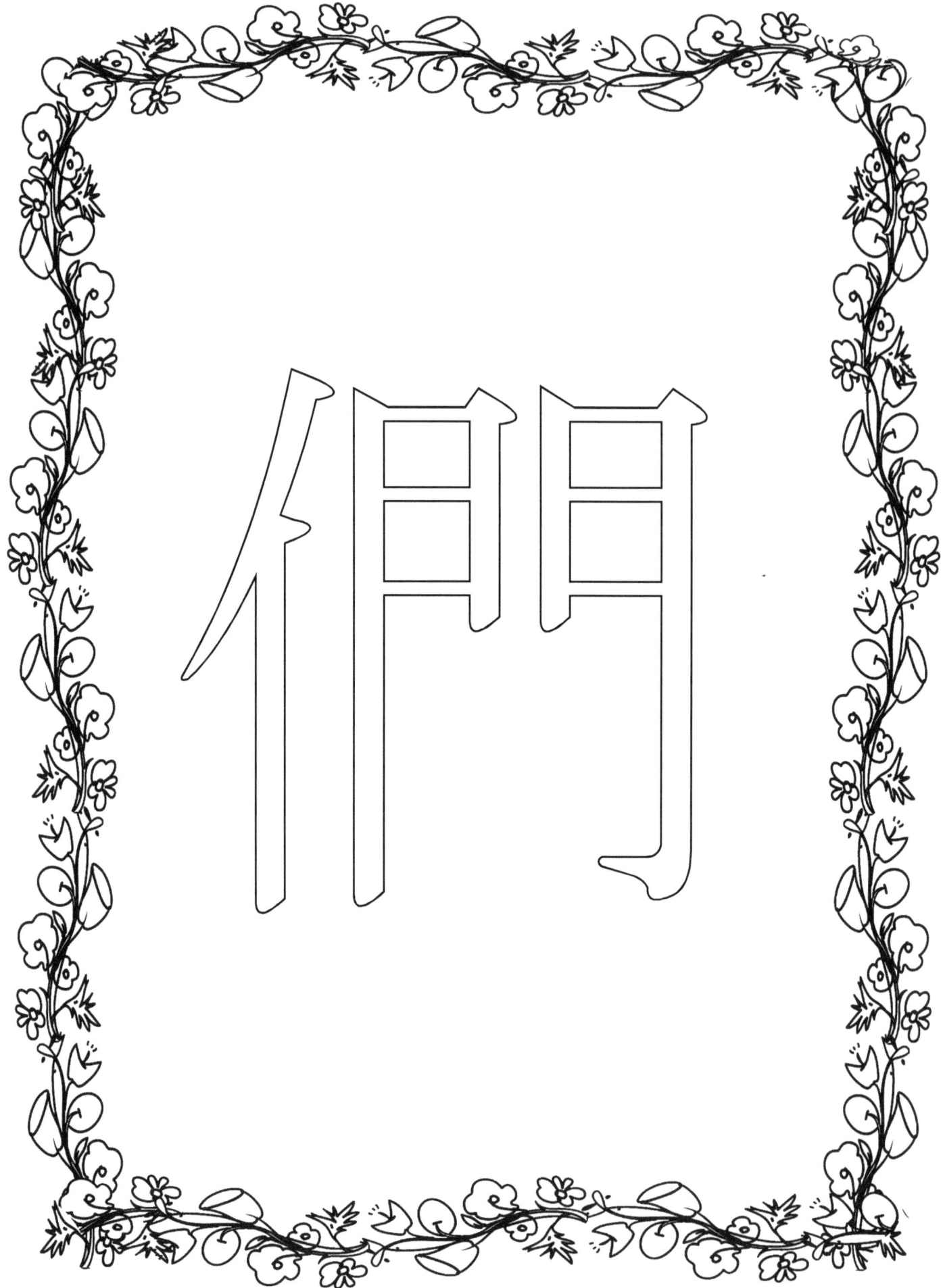

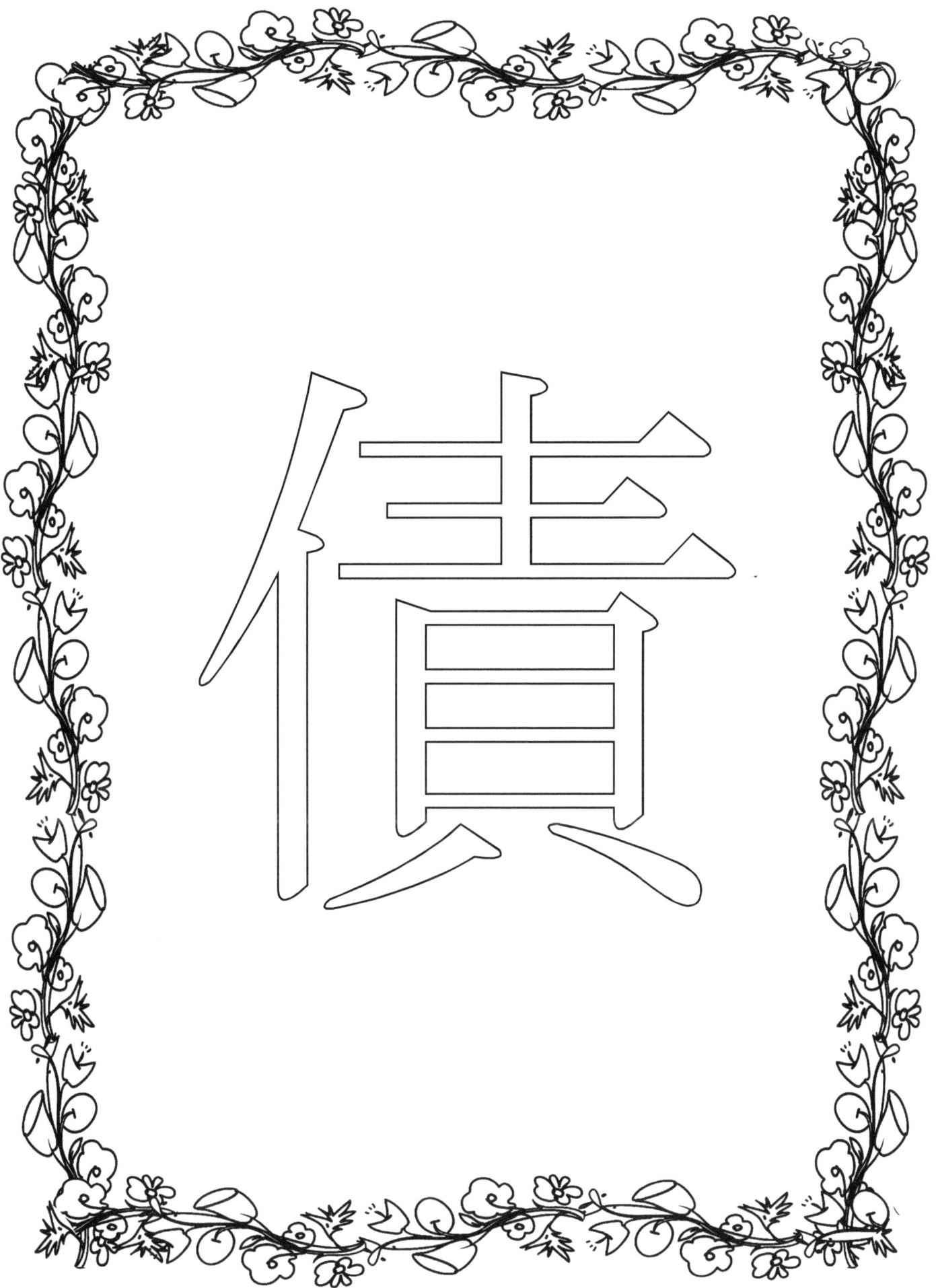

們

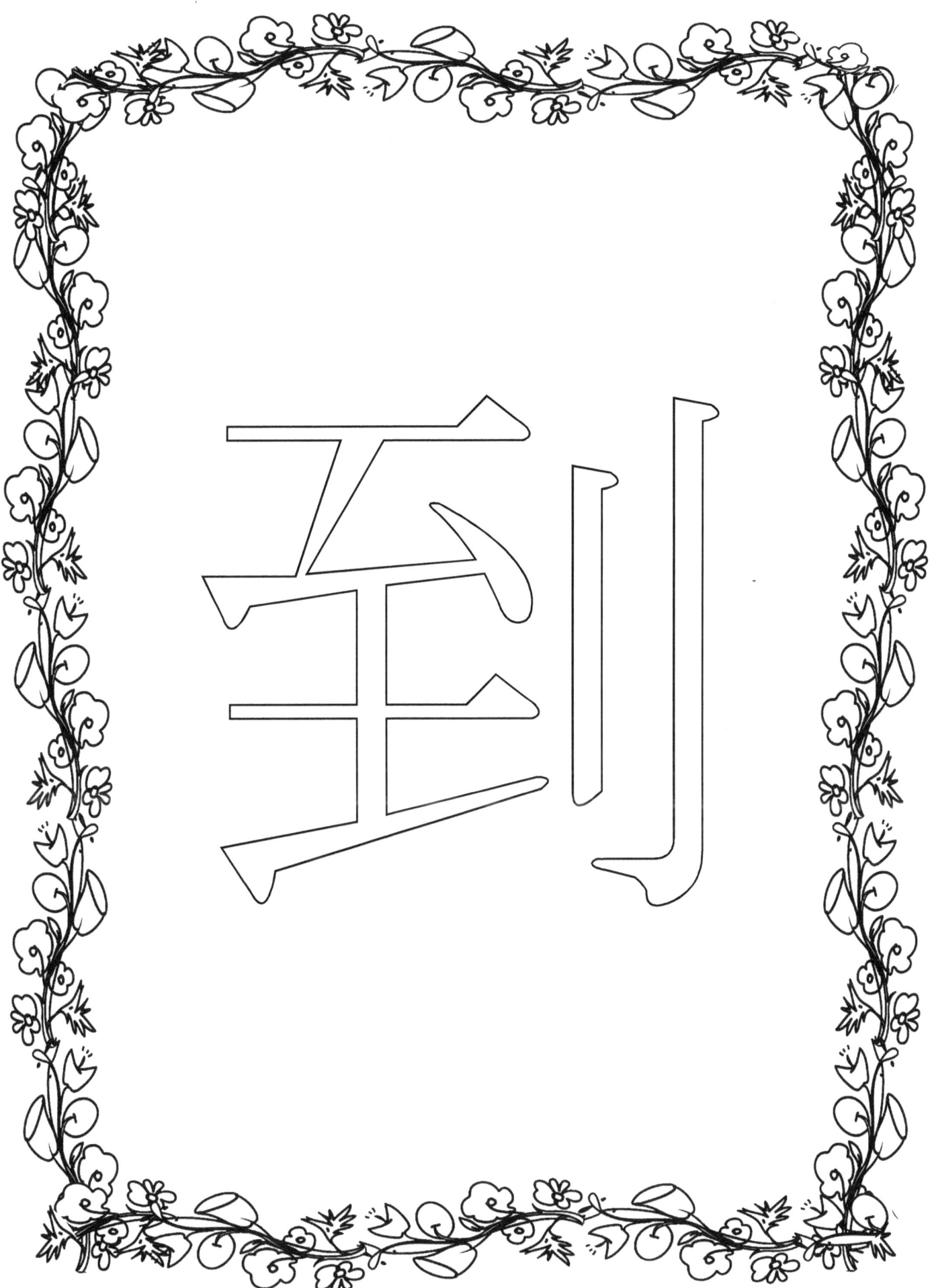

Text/Transliteration/Translation

我們在天上的父,
Wo mên zai tiên shang de fu,
Our father in heaven,

願人都尊祢的名為聖,
Yüan rên dou gou ni de ming wei sheng,
Hallowed be Thy name,

願祢的國降臨,
Yüan ni de guo jiang lin,
Thy kingdom come,

願祢的旨意行在地上,
Yuan ni de zhi yi xing zai di shang,
Thy will be done on earth,

如同行在天上。
Ru tong xing zai tian shang.
As it is in heaven.

我們日用的飲食 今日賜給我們,
Wo mên ri yong de yin shi jin ri tsi gei wo mên
Our daily bread give us today,

免我們的債
Miên wo mên de zhai
Forgive our debts

如同我們免了人的債
Ru tong wo mên mian le ren de zhai,
As we forgive our debtors

不叫我們遇見試探,
Bu jiao wo mên yu jiên shi tan,
Lead us not into temptation,

救我們脫離兇惡,
Jiu wo mên tuo li xiung er.
Deliver us from evil.

[因為國度、權柄、榮耀, 全是祢的, 直到永遠。
Yin wei guo du, chüan bing, rong yao, chüan shih ni de, zhi dao yong yuan
For the kingdom, the power, and the glory are yours, Now and forever.

阿們!
Amen!

www.ingramcontent.com/pod-product-compliance
Lightning Source LLC
Chambersburg PA
CBHW051257110526
44589CB00025B/2860